Things Are Disappearing Here

Things Are Disappearing Here

Poems

Kate Northrop

A KAREN & MICHAEL BRAZILLER BOOK
PERSEA BOOKS / NEW YORK

Persea Books, Inc.
853 Broadway
New York, NY 10003   ·

Library of Congress Cataloging-in-Publication Data

Northrop, Kate, 1969-
  Things are disappearing here : poems / Kate Northrop.
      p. cm.
  "A Karen & Michael Braziller Book."
  ISBN 0-89255-329-4 (trade pbk.)
  I. Title.

  PS3614.O78T47 2007
  811'.6—dc22

                                    2006031899

Designed by Lytton Smith
Printed in the United States of America
First edition

—for Molly Ayres

Acknowledgements

Grateful acknowledgement is made to the editors of the following magazines in which these poems first appeared, sometimes in slightly different versions:

AGNI: "The Neighbor," "Now over the Empty Apartment"

American Poetry Review: "Dive," "A Glimpse of You, a Vision," "Night, Museum Garden," "Slant, and Far Across the Sea"

Ducky IV: "The Striking Blondes"

From the Fishouse (www.fishousepoems.org): "The Film," "Sunset City"

Raritan: "The Baby," "Three Women," "Night Skiers," "View of the Farm," "The Dog," "The Ghost Crab," "Things Are Disappearing Here"

Runes Review: "Female Scarecrow"

Sewanee Theological Review: "The Pure Beauties"

32 Poems: "The Place Above the River"

Poems in this collection have also been included in *Through Which Footsteps*, winner of the 2005 West Town Press chapbook award. My thanks to the editors, Brian Young and Jenny Mueller, as this later book is a better one for their help with the first. Section II of "Three Women" was printed in a limited edition series by artist Brian Curling of Goldfinch Press. I continue to be touched by his work, by his ways of knowing the world.

Several poems would not have been written without the presences of certain people: "Three Women" is dedicated to William Kulik, "Night Skiers" to Alicia Meller, "The Burglar" to Allison Ramler and "Now over the Empty Apartment" to Jesse Rossa.

My thanks also to the Pennsylvania Council on the Arts for several Individual Artist Fellowships which granted me time and space. For criticism, conversation, patience, and support, I am grateful to and for Cynthia Clem, Jough Dempsey, Gabe Fried, Nick Ingram, Julia Levine, Ellen Wehle and Harvey Hix.

Contents

III

IV

I

The Dog

He comes leaping out of the closed door of my dreams—
a dark retriever, slick

as if he had just swum quickly across a river

and his name tags glitter
though nothing is written on them.

In the center of the living room he sits
and he persists
as flowers persist: a vase of the freshly cut

demanding in sunlight to be seen—
until I give up. Washing dishes,
pretending *nothing's there*, when I look,

the dog isn't there; he's into the field, nose
to the trail of some circling

missing thing. I call but he's off
instantly into the woods, where all day he drifts,

impossible to know, and does not get lost.

Female Scarecrow

The skirt flaps in our garden,
      that worn cotton upon which
roses were printed long ago

yet having faded, further back
      than background, are they not

more real than the remembered ones,
      those opening

summers in the hedgerow?—And still,

      however pale, visible
unlike your mother living in the house
years ago, years even

before you arrived—little tangle
      of worry—already
too late.

And tell me, what is there
to frighten now? The barn
      sails into evening,

the trees go, the road,

and waves of deer
rise from the woods toward the back
of the garden. They walk

all night, past the figure
that continues—not moving—

but hanging there.

The Reconstruction Team

reconstructs the accident—rural, roadside. They happen it
    backwards, withdraw her first whole from halved

fragments: girl/boy, shoulder/grass, crease/radio, and they station

the ducks—witnesses—as such: a collective stunned, or quacking, quacking
    yet drawn always back to the pond's green ghosts, to their one *true love*:
the newly minted rain, which runnels through the seedy cow path,

which touches ducks, lovely, regardless of the swerve
    born through weather,

through the clattering of branches to be strewn—in the gorgeous
    morning—

across field and road, the limbs wrenched
    from right position, split, yet brilliant
the bark in sunlight. Dark, glittering—

                    But first the boy,
no star or cocksure quarterback, leads his Susan
back through the parking lot, again to the car

but not directly. Pauses first, considers appearances—some smuggled rum? (Smoke
    already snaking past the median and sly, the silvered leaves.) True,

some things are mist, exist
beyond a team—lyrics perhaps, the hands. And so,

in general, one says *the guard rail* or one says *the borrowed car*, the inside of which
    is blue, not aquamarine *per se* but the light

prismed through, hovering along the edge of Susan's décolleté.

The Baby

The shadows of the couple
        enter the dark field, cross
silent as a seam

having left at the center
a white box, white
as a box

for a birthday cake. Inside,
the baby.
Abandoned there

in the tall grass,
in the night wind,

he wants for everything: food, warmth,
        a little
baby hope.

        But the world
swirls around the box. The world

like a forest goes on

and paths go on through it,
        each road leading nowhere, leading away

from the baby. Still
in the center of the field,
his breath

rises quietly. Grasses shiver.
Overhead, through trees

a sound approaches, like wings,
or this time, scissors.

Night, Museum Garden

The statues here are like the living dead
or no, these are the ones stopped

      —who cannot move about, moan
or walk—

      suspended like this
in their continuing predicaments: the horse

         in the far corner, startled,

rearing; the girl about to bathe, who turns
         toward some interruption, the woman

seated beneath the cherry tree, looking away
from what may be a grave—

Their faces this evening
      mirror clearly
what they do not face

while over the wall
      trees rustle. A few taxis

pass on the avenue, and further

the moon goes by, but again
silently, like a boat rowed over an empty pool.

Lines

The unluckiest among us fall in love
    with such a thing as a line,

and from the beginning, it goes badly.

You can bring a line into your home
    but your gestures so alarm it
it breaks into two, four,

       sixteen lines and they keep
breeding, breeding. There's no

maneuvering them. One line
    escapes you

and appears years later
aimless in the garden. If you had been wise,

you would not have fallen for a nature
so given to infidelity:

Lines always go in two directions.

I myself was once in love with a line.
    I took it to a field
and lay down next to it

whispering *Relax, we're alone*
but the line would have none of it.

      Soon night had fallen
and rising over the hill came cars, stories,

came windows through which I saw
everything as it must remain:

singular, burning, private.

The Striking Blondes

That's it, they are sick of being looked at, of maintaining the *je ne sais quoi*, the *voulez-vous*, and above all, of struggling to remain light under the weight of our gaze.

They are tired of trying to live at our level for truly, have they not always been other than us: the blondes that go by in the grass, the glossy blondes, finely tuned; the slenderest, leggy ones?

And we, who were struck dumb by the slow turn of their heads and were reminded then of our most shameful moments, weren't we always beside them, and darkly, like shadows of ships? Aren't we to blame for their refusing to be viewed, for their withdrawal into the celestial world, for the piles of empty stilettos which were our little, strappy cathedrals? And there's no picket line of course. Just us here in the city, alone, haunted, as any chorus.

The First House

keeps surfacing: a hole
    opens in the bedroom wall

where years a gas lamp burned

and the soil we'd turn into garden
turns instead to mirror-shards, bits of brick,

    a ring engraved *Cherise*. All summer
our neighbor, cheerful though unemployed, stops by
with stories: do we know

about the girl? the alley? Do we know
    what people find in outhouses

like ours, out back? She drops her voice. So *sad*,
those limbs, those infants
    pitched in—but probably

we don't have to worry, although there's a creek

buried beneath our street, and just wait, in hard rain
it runs through the cellar floor

and then we'll all have—scattering
    in the kitchen—silverfish for days.

River Park

This into which a dog appeared: always
     after 3 AM, slim, collared in strict
brilliant studs, a white Pit

     and the owner—he worked
a graveyard shift—stood at the gate,

his face drawn back
     beneath a baseball hat

while the dog tore across the lawn
     after ball, or stick—ripped them

to shreds—. Always
     after 3 AM into a place, so late,
of juxtaposition: the willows

along the river oppose
     the road; the grove

of flowering cherries
     opposes the billboard—*National Bible*—
glowing over the factory;

and in the corners of the community garden
men strange to each other

meet and pair off, face, or one's
     on his knees, anonymous, some

beautiful, or vicious, some cut with muscle
     as the dog was:

in the center of the field
and nameless then as well, so focused by flight

    she could not hear the voice
calling her in, attached to a path as flame's

    attached to gasoline, and so white she was blue
in the center of the field, there moving through.

The Neighbor

Now it's their daughter
laughing with a boy who calls from the window
something precise and obscene

to the two men crossing the park,
        carrying large instruments
in dark cases.

Snow hangs over the city

and when one man stops, shifting his weight,
the other looks at the sky.

Then they walk on, past the fountain; they go
        straight through the shadows of trees. Perhaps
they don't hear, or aren't worried by girls; perhaps

they couldn't care less, but I live here beside her

and I know that laughter made exactly of angles.
        I know her face
and her eyes that are hollow,

smooth as a place where a rock has been.

II

Three Women

I. North

The stars here are too precise,
      too pure—they pierce the sky

and without looking I know each one
glitters in the window. Once,

when we lived together
      in the city, I gave dinners;
I could look at things, people for example, flowers,

and a bloom was a bloom,

not a tragedy, not a papery flounce
lodged in time, and so, swallowed then,
      forgettable. Do you see how sick I am

of the view? Even here, especially here, it's always
my mind doing the looking,

my mind waiting for anything,
      for an arrival, a sudden event,

a cut, or a cry capable of breaking
this relentlessness. I see why
I tired you,

but I was tired also of lying. I see these fields;
I see there is no narrative arc, no *rise, rise, rise*, not even
a *you*, a still place

to put things. Just stars,
tunnels, this month, this room—

II. Prague

Wherever I go, I bring evening.

I am the sorrow of flowers that open at twilight,
sorrow of doorways and bottles,
of cats that disappear in the rustling hedge.

I am the face you saw once by the lamp in the window,
—that which almost belonged to you,

or the sudden cry from the uppermost room
and further, the attic, and then the sorrow of twilight.

Wherever I go, I am lovely, and lovely,
bring burdens: sweetness, age, evening.

III. The Lost Wife

If only our story weren't
    so ordinary: first,

pain loses its cut, its perfect

specificity, then names
    dissolve, even those I knew for you

and for our locations.
    A longing—without clear
definition—pervades

like the smell of hay
    which rising from a freshly
mowed field rises as well

from those we rode through, mist

in the vague mountains. Only scent
    travels between worlds. Real things

refuse to be called back. Still it is strange

I shouldn't further be able
to remember you, who were so often
with me. Inside the house,

in other countries. When I slept,

I knew the weight of your leg
    on mine. I had wanted
always to be there: held

down. And this is what happens:

I've become a scent myself, moving
    through the woods, a shift
—however slight—in the warm and humid air.

The Bedroom Mirror

Again it was winter, the world
      suddenly slow, and everything you said
I learned to believe.

Upstairs: our neighbor shuffled, always dusting—beatific. I knew
already her reprimands. *Lucky enough*
to be here. That was her

philosophy. But Neighbor!

What of the tasseled bikes, the mitts and bats
      assumed into dark garages?

What of the empty street spreading away
like something spilt?
      Indifferent, clear, too clean—

Oh, she didn't believe in drivel.
People just won't be pleased.

True, true. But what I saw
mornings there in the mirror
      was first my body,

then moving over it, your body,

      then above us,
in sky, the highest reaches of the elm,
stripped branches

      which birds sailed through sailing by.

The Visitor

All day they multiply—the lurid plurals—area codes,
    chores, clouds:

quarter the chicken, mince into piles
    the stalks of parsley
while boys from town boom by in trucks

       that river up the road dust. Nights
are cold, are speeding vehicles—and the bottles tossed out

spin from the hands, rise
       until the earth turns

and they thud back into the mud-husks. Good bottles,

they will moan in the morning like bones,
       wash up in the gutter run-off
like the remnants of a dream: *I was lost*

   in the kitchen. Something overhead, dripping. A man
      drove his fork into a plate

or like the bedroom after sex: his pillow, then mine.
     Thigh-highs back
in the thigh-high drawer. All day

     I pair this
to that: door to jamb, foot
to shoe, grain over the gate

to a flurry of chickens but later
     I am waiting,

at the sink
with my hands under the spigot, under the water drawn
     from darkness

into the order of the house, or on the sleeping porch

at twilight, I am waiting
without a letter, a ticket, for you,

who by the curve of the woods
        and at the lip of the frayed lake, are like twilight:
when leaving, appear there—

Dive

More difficult by night, you must
          make yourself up in tank & mask
and from the stern, ease

          into the water, into a place that does not

readily appear, does not
assume you: suited-up and numbed by gloves, strapped

          to a machine. And what did you think?
That as it is
in the shallows of sunlight,

          you might pick a point—the teeming reef, flickering

of an Angel fish—and focused there,
          arrive before your body? No,

this is the world which for once

          does not believe in you.
This is the anchor line, and though you can barely see,
          pin your eyes to the braided rope. The algaed frays,

thicker now beneath your hand, twist
          and loom. Here is the lamp,

the beams of which disperse into surge & emptiness,
into indifference of the gravest depth, and yet

descending, is this not
          what you always wanted, to be

as pure mind, reading closely, a verb

without responsibility to object? Are you not—stripped
   of all accompaniment and falling

toward the world you've dreamed of—
                  almost a perfect

cleanliness, almost the soul, if not for your hand—now yours,
   now alien—sliding over the rope?

October

Standing by the pond,
he wavered over the pond
therefore I believed
though each morning I watched
the world return: slow
body of a hedgerow, then surfacing,
the gray-green lawn
across which the dog chain lay, I saw,
like a dropped garden tool.

Standing by the road,
he'd gone down the road—winter
already a blur in the eye—
but first, the fractures of daylight:
doors slammed
further down the street
and one neighbor yelled goodbye—*Bye!*—
and one drove off cursing
in a swirl of shitty road-dust.

Such racket. I had to keep
night close. What I knew once,
I remember. I hold in my palm
like a stone. Do you see?
I imagine the world
pure, all dross burnt away,
and when I feel myself slip,
I press that cold stone
here against my throat.

Aspens

You would say they are white
They are not white
Although their secret is
A private cleanliness

You would say the sound
Their leaves make is slight
It is not slight the sound
Of the leaves is the sound

Of very small stones
Rolled under the tide
A sound that's kept you awake
On certain nights haunted

As if on a back stair
Or here at the window
Drawn again by the meadow
Thin transparent cold

A Glimpse of You, a Vision

Late afternoons, through Florida's blue shades, I saw you everywhere,
                                            an effervescence
        blanking out the tips of the lime blossoms, then skirting

the darkening street. And the girl next door
        playing Chopin over and over—why didn't you return

at least to one of us? I kept silent a long time

        believing, given room, you would appear. Instead,

I heard the passengers leaving the train, the train
        leaving the station. No. I heard the swing-set

out back—strange to me still, creaking.

The Ghost Crab

Evenings he runs up the path
    leading down to the sea

and waits on the porch
quietly, under a chair in the corner.
He breathes

and leaves turn into autumn, turn
    like the guests that have left:
silver, ringing through the woods.

And when he arrives
    the shoreline below—that glittery curve

of sand & stone—rises.
It hovers between two worlds, like prayer,
    or longing,

between the darkness of land
and the darkness of water. It is other

then either. It is something else
    entirely—

You may go down
and standing at the edge, listen

as if listening could draw the night
    finally into the body

but you will not be able to remain, not
    in that emptiness: the cool on your arms

is the cool remove of moonlight.

The Burglar

By going in, he learns the integrity
     of surfaces: where a house is tightly knit,

where it least resists, and once inside he is

your opposite. Listening
in your living room, he hears fields

of wheat, and hillside, the rustle
     of women, corn
but there's no time for that. Quickly,

     he's vanished
and then for weeks how awful in daylight
your belongings look: the coats

on hooks; the drapes,

dumb, vulnerable; and the piano,
     its arrangement of photographs—each face
in position, smiling, smiling

as if at him, for whom you listen in the night, and miss—

The Countess

I've begun with four corpses thrown from a wall
    into the path of wolves,
and then again with the bodies of girls.

A stream running through a field. Moonlight on a ruined garden.

Or started later with drifts, with a sense of events moved through air:
                                    one afternoon,
    a summer especially warm, the mountains, say, east
of what was known once

as Czechoslovakia, grit and sunlight, a kitchen stunned by heat & cherries,
    the skin, the dark flesh simmering
in an old pan, the flame beneath breaking forms

down into preserves, and outside, the smell of the day's laundry, sheets
    blown over the earth not yet scorched, just

turning through years, through distance: wind-driven, the wave of diesel fumes,
                                    a truck
    idling along an empty road, then music rising
from an empty room.

Or I've started at the edge of a market—a pigeon
    fixed to the asphalt by a stick two boys
drive through its iridescent neck. Statistically

murderers are men and so once, were boys, still

I could begin again with a girl, with Elizabeth Báthory, who grows
beautiful, a Countess who goes *gynocidally berserk*,

but first, at eleven years of age in the seventeenth century, hides in the castle
    and from behind a column, watches, as the morning light
clears the field, a man being sewn

into the slit belly of a horse. And it's fucked up alright: the gypsy
who had sold his only daughter knew all night
        tomorrow I am to be sewn alive

into the slit belly of a horse and tore at himself, imagining guts, warmth, as the
                                                    scavengers
        started arriving, already at the blurred edge of the woods,

and Elizabeth Báthory, also awake, lay in her bed
        listening to what rose through her window: his prayers,
his strange moans.

—⌁—

As others have depicted her, Itsvan, an early Impressionist: she is seated in a chair
                                            —her head
        thrown back—and the chair is positioned in drifts of snow
so she may best behold the view: three girls stripped

led out of doors, doused in water, rolled in snow
from which they try to rise, and almost do: each face

surfacing at the crest of pain. All turn and upward curve, their forms
        stretch and end in the reach of hands, of arms. The closest, at the Countess's

feet, is screaming, her mouth so wide it's as if
what felt pain and was particular

could find a way out; could attach itself to something loving
        and sudden; be lifted free

from named abstraction—peasant, girl—and leave the body
        before the body itself was left,
shaking outside, freezing in the snow.

—⌁—

34

I've read each legend. Evidently she had been, before her marriage, with many men,
   promiscuous at sixteen and delivered a daughter
they hushed right up.

She was literate, compelling,
independent. She kept her name and was in the seventeenth century

too quickly out of mourning, scandalous
   at the court. There's the possibility

of reason: a servant girl, combing the Countess's hair,
   pulled too tight. She was slapped until her blood fell
and when wiped from the Countess's hand, it left the skin

luminous. Or there's a stretch of woods—tamaracks & birches—
   through which Báthory rides with suitors. There's an old hag

looking up from a path the wind has swept with leaves

who speaks: "Take care. Listen, soon you will look like me,
   then what will you do?"

In the castle, imagine,
hours at the mirror. She was listening. "What you have now
   you will no longer have. Years. Youth."

Lines would arrive. Slowly, without clearly having happened.

They would mark her.
   She said prayers.

For hours, incantations. *Soon.*

—⚭—

First it was only at the castle, underground at Čachtice, then further,
    with her eldest aunt, at that castle,
then in Vienna,

then on a street known later as the one where blood runs,

behind St. Stephens in a house bordered on one side
by a wealthy family, and on the other

by a monastery. In the evening: iron maidens, lines of knives.
Then one after another, waves
    of tin cups the monks

hurled against the wall—a shower of forks, spoons—
    and their hands pounding at screams, then pounding
at a silence born through.

—⟋⟍⟋—

Listen, the victims were servants, hired girls
and nobility could do what nobility wished
    with discipline, and Báthory did, over and over until

the corpses became *the corpse problem*.
    I've begun with the spaces she found

to toss them: silos, streams, the edge of a field. In the town cemetery,
    hasty graves. Shadows in the garden.

I've begun with the only boy involved, deformed & poor, known

only as *boy*, Fičzkó, and begun again at the border of woods

or later, in an empty square, years later, with the stink of diesel, with a boy I knew
who whispered in my ear *Listen, I didn't fuck her;*

Listen, she was ugly—

—ɷ—

Afterwards, her name—Báthory—became forbidden. Throughout field and town,
in houses even, you could not say it. Not in the streets,

not in the fluttering market.

—ɷ—

She liked those
        with the largest breasts

and afterward, she numbered each girl in a journal, noting disappointments,
"she was too small."

Listen, it was the paleness of the inner arms. It was *clear brow and rising curve*
        —their light-giving

living skin, the layers unending without age or inscription; it was this craving
        which is like that one: to enter through resistance
into what moves beneath—life, voice,

blood—*Take care. Soon.* Once with her teeth she even
        she tore into the flesh of one breast
—*she was too small.*

Or here, again at the end: it's December, the night of the raid,
        and the four corpses in mid-air
are falling from the heights of the castle

into the path of wolves. The authorities

are hours away and Báthory must change her soaked clothes before carrying on
and Fičzkó mops up the blood

because the last victim, Dulcina, a *strapping girl*
is taking too long. Because this one, it is written,
    just would not die.

—ɷ—

She was a Countess; she was not
        executed. She was noble, she did not
stand trial. There was

a bargain, a communication through letter: *You do not deserve*

        to see the light of the Lord. You are like
an animal. I condemn you
to imprisonment for life in your castle. So someone

walls over the room, walls over the door, and there are two
ventilation slits, one opening

through which jailers pass food. Again through letter: *Shadows will envelop you.*
    When you disappear from this world, you will never again

reappear here. I've begun
with one particular jailer, he who will discover her
    lying face down on the floor—like any old

movie drunk, but dead—he is young and had only thought, since she was still
    so beautiful that he might bend down

and pressing his face to the wall, get a better look.

—ɷ—

What you have now you will no longer have. Years.

38

Youth. Over six hundred
and fifty. All those girls. Iridescent

in her fever. Like grit,
        like vegetables in sunlight:
forms, flesh. *Years,*

        youth. Soon.

What then to do with these horses? With girls?
        What with trucks
and the slight path their leaving has left

        in wheat, in the rising sun-lit field?

Museum Diorama:

I'm not like you. I exist
    where wind's implicit, my ear
cocked to it, my ear

        trained beyond the schools of temporary children
further to the whir

of the fan, the meter,
    its steady click. And you? What you have done

with your hands? They hang there: dumb
    encumbrances—

I won't look. And even with the aid of this bowed
    insulting background—haze

of hope & atmosphere—I won't

be located. Your gaze falls short;
    it leaks away,

and I see what's happened: you've lost your feel for strict
precisions, for contraptions. What do you know

of *drawn arrow*? of *spent shell*? They've gone the way
    of metaphor now, of preservation, as have I, reduced like this finally

to language, to standing in the place
    of something else. But at least I'm free
to remain here. You must not—

you must return to your cars and coats,
to the roads stacked with traffic,

but when you step from the garage this evening,

as you approach the lights of the house,
listen to me:

You can't forget
everything. I called you once

and you followed. In this way, you were whole.

Slant, and Far Across the Sea

Listen, everyone in a room
wants

a division, a crack at a girl.
Just keep

one eye out;
don't lean toward windows, don't drink
greedily like that.

And when you pass through a room, smile
directly, *at* someone

even if
they seem to be engaged
in conversation—tell me, who's

completely engaged?—

              and the transaction
shall act as an anchor. Soon you will circle
through *turn*, through *give me*

your attention; you will see each face
as something immaculate,

a study of weather
in the distance, a square of rain slanting down

to where it storms across the sea (though there
dark swells are, waves cracking open—). And if sometime

it surfaces, that particular

memory, the turn
down a gone hallway, or how you shamed yourself

once in somebody's kitchen (—the sunlight

filtering in) let a secret steady your resolve. Maintain,
maintain. To appear

is to escape.

Now over the Empty Apartment

You in the door look back
    and are no longer there,

although that is the hall
    through which you walked a hundred times
thinking *well, what of it?*—awake

    in the middle of the night—

and that is the window where the sky drew back and night came on,

    where the planes banked in
scheduled and flashing from the west—

    Your hand was pulling shut the shade
and mornings, your hand pulled it up again

though you are not there, you in the door going over the days,
    going as a wave goes, that is

nowhere, and all your lovers now? Those real,
    imagined? The sad,
gratified sighs?

    All that while,
through the evenings, didn't something
    quietly call,

something off in the marginal light,

in the vapor through which
    the faces of passengers dimmed

and flickered? That slight
    rivering, insistent

beneath the blare of the television, beneath you as well, at the surface

busy with addresses, with pictures & books. You crowded the place,
　　you in the door

who looking back now—over the hallway, the shine
　　of the relentless floor—

can no longer be sure

you are the person indeed who had that body
　　and lived days in it there.

IV

The Place Above the River

The house is empty and girls go in.
They drift through hours in the summer.
Across the river, music begins:

Love, it's summer. The closed homes open.
The docks are decked with lights. But further
the house is empty and girls go in

to light their lovely cigarettes; they listen
closely to the woods. Leaves? A slowing car?
Across the river, music begins

where wives are beautiful still, and thin
(in closets their dresses hang, sheer as scarves)
while the house is empty and the girls go in,

shimmering, to swallow vodka, or gin,
which burn, and to lean from where the windows were.
Across the river, music begins

and will part waves of air. *Now. Then.*
The season's criminal, strict and clear.
The house is empty. Girls go in.
Across the river, music begins.

Her Apology, and Lament

Blue fields, blue shades
    and his new resolve: each could be

what the other wanted.

—⁂—

Early it was *come for cocktails*: a shaker full of vodka,
    and the bones of the vegetable garden

barely there: stray blossom, dropped stalk—

Once, a moving recitation. Then, predictably, all dissolving.

—⁂—

        Early, in the truck & heels,
            here of course, and why not—

the rest of the world

receding like color from the cornfield, like details
    from a story: stockings, corn silk,

proposals, road-dust, heels.

—⁂—

Summers, always the clatter of blackbirds
    and pie plates,

afternoons long in the room while shadows

drove the last of the light
across the sloped field

and once, in autumn, in the middle of the night,
the dog gone off,

the white dog a weird blue, beyond the garden,
        his nose in the deer carcass,

his nose in the clean bones, and the whole scene

        made apparent by moonlight.

—⬚—

Nights into years, and then what? This?

You tell me   Go on

        In the face of the faded garden,
the cold singe of the lake,

in the wrecked arrangement of what
        had been a deer,

then what? Nothing?

—⬚—

A knock at the door.
        It's the water rising in the basement.
        It's your mother, Regina,

but whose dress is that?

        It's the ghost of the butchered deer.
It's your old fantasy, *C'mon, fuck me, harder*
It's the motorcycle your brother

spun out on, the interstate
frozen through Pennsylvania; it's guitar,
a shaving of ice, then the red-wings

overhead again. It's the new room—*something
for you to write in*—with a view

of the edge of a shimmering lake.

View of the Farm

Although intact, half-abstract
    like the deck of a ship

where the diver hovers underwater

although the properties of water
    will not allow water to move
as quietly around the farm

as moonlight moves—like a stranger,
without striking anything. It pools

around the pond, around the base of each reed.
    It turns road
into still river. When daylight returns

we'll have the lie—names,
    clear relationships—
but not yet, not at this

open moment: the house, the attic windows blanked out

    and the chickens asleep
under the dark peak of the coop. Only here and there
a stray cluck, a slight rustle,

then silence again,
    through which the creek rises,
through which footsteps run

above the silvery lawn.

The Lovers·

They are somewhere
        just beyond the realm of the painting

because these are their clothes
        cast-off at the edge of a sea
repeating itself

until emptied of meaning, emptied
        like clothes themselves, and yet
the lovers attend

        those things fallen on the bluff: a shoe

unlaced, overturned; the drape
of an opened blouse; a hat resting
        against the stark

edge of a tree, that wind-twisted moment
        of punctuation. Beside the still

rise of the ocean you see
        the lovers are absent there

in the late afternoon light
        and in that which sways overhead
darkening the grass.

Things Are Disappearing Here

Things are disappearing here: a pale light
    spreads over the sea beneath which

X drops, falls back to the blind
    silences, to the undeveloped

secret fish which have been abandoned there
    and grow vicious.
And *things are disappearing*

also in the country. Already the roads
twist into the distance, rise
    into columns of smoke

and in the parking lots of a discount store,
    a sedan explodes. Then it happens that our fathers
fly off, a whole flotilla fills the sky,

their jackets and ties flapping

like the pages of books the never read. Our fathers
    are disappearing yet they are not

ashamed. See, all things go: at the edge of the city, dogs run off,
they tear themselves from their lines

and in the middle of the night,
from neighborhoods more trenchant than ours, we hear their barks,
those clear openings that come to us

over the schoolyard, the homes boarded up, and then
    in through windows. The sound of the missing dogs

for a while survives, and that is just enough
to cheer us.

The Film

Come, let's go in.
The ticket-taker
has shyly grinned
and it's almost time,
Lovely One.
Let's go in.

The wind tonight's too wild.
The sky too deep,
too thin. Already it's time.
The lights have dimmed.
Come, Loveliest.
Let's go in

and know those bodies
we do not have to own, passing
quietly as dreams, as snow.
Already leaves are falling
and music begins.
Lovely One,

It's time.
Let's go in.

Night Skiers

Now they are falling
     through a system of dreams—and appearing

out of the pines, they descend

     on trails blue & luminous as bones
photographed in the body, and what's clear

     from a distance is the revelation
of miniatures: they have gone up

in order to fall, as do the names of those
     we no longer know, as do headlights crossing the wall
of a kitchen beyond which the wind

ruffles rows of dead corn, and the skiers

dropping easily this evening through the lines of structure—trees,
     lifts—pause once or twice, hinged

in a parallel turn, but do not care
     —not now—to listen to those
faint scratches in the buried dirt—so they land,

     and cutting in, carrying on, are they not
beautifully suited?—to descend like this,

returning again to the base
     and to the lover who is half-
imagined, and waiting there.

Sunset City

Say the empties go out.
A girl in the window wavers.

Say the old dog rattles
attached to the back of the yard, and here comes
the holy ice-cream truck,

      that rhyme & cling paused
where children spin. And say, the empties

gone out (you've rinsed the bottles, the mouth
      of each bottle) and the girl's

turned in a window beyond which the dog, that pile of bones,

keeps rattling, say the light of the streetlamp
pools over the names, again

      etched in cement—*Brianne, Amber*—and how quiet

it gets. Sunday in the city. The man at the corner
      closes shop.

Down the street goes his car, goes
the echo of his music
      and up comes the bus, local

in the evening, turning toward 10th, the windows

filthy, streaked where you see yourself
      barely but there
drawing away in the gloaming.

The Pure Beauties

There they go—flying
    out of our hands

and for all the world looking like our memory
of leaves turned on the pond into boats
and then, of the boats themselves,

the horizon's white sails
disappearing, and steadily.

There they go—the pure beauties—
    tra la la,

each one perfectly alone
as a balloon is, as a small child,

they who never even knew of us
standing here in love
with the boats, our hearts, and losing them.

About the Author

Kate Northrop is the author of a previous collection, *Back Through Interruption*, winner of the 2001 Stan and Tom Wick Poetry Prize. Recipient of several grants from the Pennsylvania Council on the Arts, she has published poems in many periodicals, including *AGNI*, *Raritan*, and *American Poetry Review*. Associate Professor of English at West Chester University in Pennsylvania, she divides her time between Philadelphia and Laramie, Wyoming.